Lana TURNER

Lana TURNER

A SILVER VALLEY CHILDHOOD

CYNTHIA ACKLEY NUNN

AMERICA
THROUGH TIME®
ADDING COLOR TO AMERICAN HISTORY

To Judy, the smiling spirit of the child who was Wallace's own.

America Through Time is an imprint of Fonthill Media LLC
www.through-time.com
office@through-time.com

Published by Arcadia Publishing by arrangement with Fonthill Media LLC
For all general information, please contact Arcadia Publishing:
Telephone: 843-853-2070
Fax: 843-853-0044
E-mail: sales@arcadiapublishing.com
For customer service and orders:
Toll-Free 1-888-313-2665

www.arcadiapublishing.com

First published 2020

Copyright © Cynthia Ackley Nunn 2020

ISBN 978-1-63499-204-6

All rights reserved. No part of this publication may be reproduced, stored in a retrieval system or transmitted in any form or by any means, electronic, mechanical, photocopying, recording or otherwise, without prior permission in writing from Fonthill Media LLC

Typeset in Mrs Eaves XL Serif Narrow
Printed and bound in England

Please note that all photos are credited to the author unless otherwise stated.

Contents

	Acknowledgments	6
	Introduction	7
1	It Started With a Dance	9
2	Just Call Me Judy	16
3	In Her Footsteps	33
4	217 Bank Street—A Brief History	68
5	The San Francisco Years	85
	Want More? Video Tours	92
	About the Author	93
	More by Cynthia Ackley Nunn	94

Acknowledgments

I owe many thanks to those who helped me in the creation of this book. First and foremost, I offer my sincerest gratitude to Fonthill Media, Arcadia Publishing, and The History Press for believing in me and making this book possible in the first place. The entire team, from the publishers, editors, and designers to marketing, advertising, and printing have all been wonderful to work with. My only regret is that I was so excited with the first three books being accepted that I was remiss in thanking them before now. Special thanks go to Susan Walker for allowing me access to Lana's childhood home in Wallace, to Richard Caron for making it happen, John Schehrer of Joplin, Missouri, for granting me permission to use the rare images of early Tar River and Picher, Oklahoma, and to the University of Idaho, Special Collections and Archives, for the use of early images of Burke and Wallace, Idaho. The professional assistance and friendliness of Olivia Wikle, Courtney Berge, and Amy Thompson made the permission process easy and pleasant. Last, but definitely not least, special thanks go to Donna MacDonald of Texas, great-great-granddaughter of Fred Viele and Mable Cora Bean, and great-granddaughter of Irene Viele Clark. Donna went through old family photos and letters of the Viele family to share in this book.

Introduction

In 1937, an unknown actress named Julia Jean Turner hit the public consciousness with her debut in the movie *They Wont Forget*. Just twelve short minutes featuring the bouncy, bubbly brunette teen would launch her into a nearly fifty-year career as one of the world's most famous, memorable and highest paid actresses. Overnight, this sixteen-year-old school girl became known as the "Sweater Girl," an image that she would spend many years trying to outrun and leave behind.

Her lifestyle and early on-screen personas would lead to nicknames or labels that were equally loaded with sexual connotations: Sex Symbol, Goddess of the Silver Screen, Bombshell and, before the age of nineteen, Queen of the Night Clubs, due to her party girl image. It would take many years for Lana to land roles that had more substance.

Lana's personal life was equally filled with drama, broken marriages and scandal. The expectations and duties of Hollywood also caused conflicts with her responsibilities as a mother to her one child by actor and restaurateur, Steve Crane.

Nearly everyone knows about Lana Turner the actress. Numerous books and articles have been written about her and her rise to fame in the dream factory that is Hollywood. However, before she was a star of the silver screen, she was a little girl of the Silver Valley, with innocent hopes and dreams. Yet very little has been written about her pre-California childhood in the North Idaho Panhandle towns of Burke and Wallace. Details and facts are sketchy. Lana provided very little biographical information about her early years, and what she shared has been found to be not quite the truth as it really was, but the truth she was taught to believe. Other writers have not bothered to take the time to research, just regurgitating the same false stories, while others have not just retold minor mistakes, but have completely mangled the facts.

This book won't provide any Earth-shattering revelations, nor will it be yet another retelling of all the dirt from Lana's turbulent Hollywood years. Instead, it will be a journey back to the beginning, to before she was born, providing little known facts, revealing some insights, and setting the record straight with truth. Best of all, this book will take you on a visual tour of the same streets and buildings that Julia Jean Turner, the child, knew before she became Lana the Sex Symbol. We are fortunate that the town of Wallace, most of which has been designated on the National Historic Register, endures as it looked to her young eyes. Surely it was as much a magical place then as it is today.

Above left: Lana Turner on a 1930s issue of a BAT Modern Beauties Series 6 tobacco card. Makes one wonder if this was a deliberate play on her childhood in Wallace, Idaho.

Above right: Lana Turner on a 1940s World War II-era EKC postcard. She has metamorphosed from the wholesome-girl-from-Idaho look to the more glamorous and polished look of Hollywood.

1

It Started With a Dance

Father John, who preferred to be called Virgil or Virgie, was born September 11, 1894, to Robert Joseph Turner & Mary Annette (Nettie) Quillen in the small town of Mount Pleasant, Tennessee, where, a year after his birth, brown phosphate rock was found in the area. Soon, the town boasted ten phosphate mining companies, which provided the majority of employment opportunities available to men in the area. It is most likely here where John Turner first learned the mining trade as a young man. In 1900, John's father was a miner and his mother was employed as a cook. By 1910, Robert and Mary Turner had managed to purchase a small home farm in the village of Palestine, TN, located somewhere between Hampshire Road and Hohenwald. Farming must not have proven as successful as the Turner family had hoped, leading to a move for the large family from Tennessee to Webb City, Missouri, where we find them residing by 1917, with father Robert again working in the mines, where zinc and lead were the biggest producers. The WWI Draft Registration for that same year shows that Lana's father had registered on June 5, 1917. He was described as medium height and stout build, with blue eyes and light brown hair. He listed his occupation as miner, with parents financially dependent on him. His attempts to be exempted from registering failed and no Certificate of Exemption was granted. It was off to the Front for John Virgil Turner, to do his service in WWI. After returning from duty he decided to leave the home of his parents and move to Tulsa, Oklahoma, where he had taken up a new occupation as a baker in a local bakery.

Lana's mother, Mildred Francis Cowan, was born on February 12, 1904, in Lamar, Arkansas, to Arthur Willis Cowan and Julia Ann Cullum. Sadly, Mildred was left motherless five months after her birth, when her mother would die due to RH factor complications. Mildred's maternal grandmother also died from this same complication, leaving Mildred's mother Julia motherless at a very young age. This tells us that Mildred, her mother and her maternal grandmother were all RH negative blood types. What's interesting is that I am not finding any other children that these women gave birth to previously. Generally, a first pregnancy does not produce these complications, even if there is an RH factor incompatibility. Most of these cases tend to occur with a later pregnancy. In any case, Lana and her mother would both worry about this during their own pregnancies.

In 1910, Mildred was living in the home of her great-aunt Mary Cullum Walden in Pittsburg, Arkansas. I believe this was a sister of her maternal grandmother.

By 1917, Mildred was living with her father again. Either he felt able to care for a thirteen-year-old on his own, or the remarriage of her great-aunt caused a shift in housing circumstances. Arthur's registration for the WWI Draft Registration in 1917 tells us that they were residing in Tar River, Oklahoma, but his employment as a teamster was through George More, ore buyer, in Webb City, Missouri. I wonder why he chose to move to Tar River with his young daughter? At that time, it was a new town, just recently founded in 1913. It was also a lead and zinc mining town with a reputation for being on the wild and boisterous side. Vice and corruption were rife in this town full of dance halls, gambling dens, speakeasies, pool halls and most likely a few brothels. Lana's mother had an early crash course in the type of life and conditions she would find herself living under during her years of marriage to Lana's father. Records do not exist to tell us whether or not Mildred's father had a live-in maid to look after his daughter, if they lived in their own house, or if they were in a boarding house where he left his young daughter to her own devices while he was working long hauls as a teamster. Tar River's name was changed to Cardin in 1920. Now, it is a ghost town, located in the Tar Creek Superfund, due to contamination from the lead and zinc mines.

Sometime before 1920, Arthur moved his daughter to Picher, Oklahoma, where he also acquired a new wife, Florence. Arthur was still employed as a teamster. Picher was also founded as a town in 1913 during the lead and zinc mine boom. It can be assumed that Mildred lived with them in their rented house on Vantage Street. Now, nothing remains here. Like Tar River/Cardin, Picher also became a ghost town due to contamination from the mines and is now considered to be one of the most toxic towns in America.

In her autobiography titled *Lana, the Lady, the Legend, the Truth*, Lana claims that her maternal grandfather Arthur was a mining engineer who often took his daughter Mildred with him on mine inspection tours, and that while visiting Picher for one of these inspections, she met Lana's father, John Virgil Turner, in a roof-garden restaurant, where he asked the then-fifteen-year-old Mildred to dance. They fell deeply in love that very day and married soon after. While this is a nice romantic story, the facts say otherwise, since we know from census records that Mildred and family were already living in Picher, and her father was a teamster, not a mine inspector. Lana also stated that her father was from Montgomery, Alabama, when in fact he was from Tennessee. Was she deliberately trying to hide the facts of her parent's history? Probably not. Many people have stated in various publications, including Lana herself, that her mother Mildred was tight-lipped about discussing the family history, even with her own daughter and granddaughter. I have found no evidence of a restaurant with a roof-garden, but that isn't to say that one didn't exist in Picher. A number of possibilities exist for how Lana's parents may have actually met. Her father was a teamster who was employed by a Webb City, Missouri, company. It is conceivable that at times young Mildred accompanied her father on his hauls and became familiar with John Virgil Turner while he still lived in Webb City. With all of the new mining going on in Oklahoma, maybe John decided to try his luck in Picher, and met the young Mildred at that time. On January 5, 1920, John and Mildred eloped in Miami, Oklahoma, where they were married by Justice of the Peace John W. Kieff. Witnesses were Karl N. Sweem and C. E. Lee. Mildred lists her place of residence as Picher, but John was residing in Tulsa. This makes me believe that there was more to the story of the relationship between the fifteen-year-old Mildred and the twenty-six-year-old John Turner. Lana has stated in her book that Mildred's father did not approve of their relationship, which acted as a catalyst, causing the couple to elope. Were there other circumstances involved? Maybe. Is it possible that Mildred was already pregnant? Certainly. We cannot discount the possibility that Mildred was already pregnant with Julia Jean (Lana), or even a first pregnancy that ended up as a miscarriage. Do we have any proof of this? Sadly, no—at least not at this time.

On January 14, 1920, nine days after their marriage, we see them enumerated together for the first time as a couple in the Federal Census. It states that they resided at a boarding house located at 8 ½ N. Main Street, Tulsa, Oklahoma. Virgil listed his occupation as baker in a bakery. Nothing remains of this building. It is now just an empty lot. It was probably in these early Missouri and Oklahoma mining towns where Lana's father picked up his gambling habit that would later cause the family so much instability and financial difficulties.

Somewhere between Tulsa, Oklahoma, in 1920 and North Idaho in 1921 is where our story of Julia Jean Turner, AKA Lana, begins.

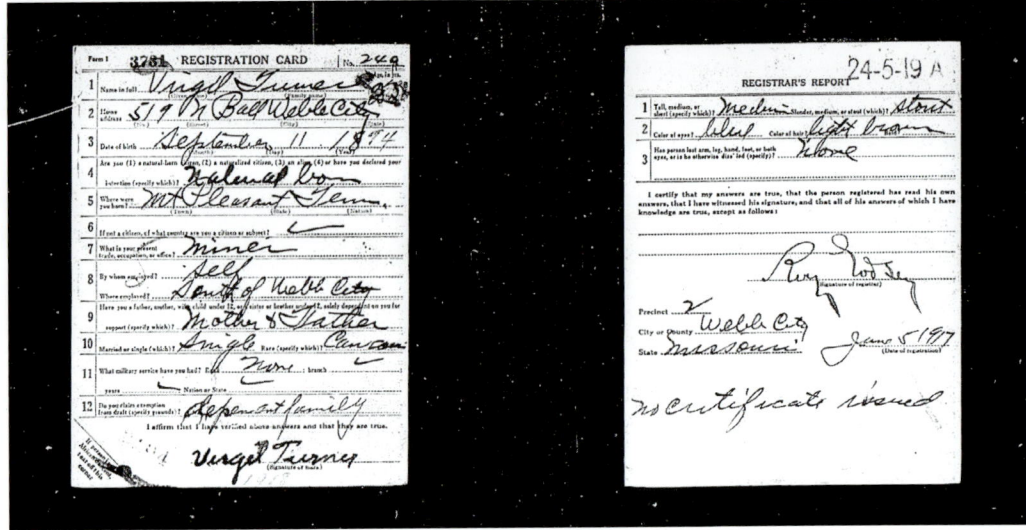

WWI Draft Registration for John Virgil Turner. [*United States World War I Draft Registration Cards, 1917-1918*]

Webb City, Missouri, *circa* 1912, showing Allen Street, which was a main business hub. These streets would have been very familiar to Lana's father as a young man about town.

OPPOSITE PAGE:

Top: Inside a lead and zinc mine in Webb City, Missouri, *circa* 1908. These are the same working conditions that Lana's father and paternal grandfather would have labored in. [*B. C. Wanglin, Publisher, Webb City, MO.*]

Middle: Tar River Grocery & Supply Company, *circa* 1913. During its heyday, Tar River boasted anywhere from eighteen to twenty grocery stores. [*John Schehrer, Joplin, Missouri, https://schehrer2.homestead.com/Cardin_2.html*]

Tar River, Oklahoma mining district, *circa* 1915. These shanties and the general run-down appearance of the area shows that those who lived here dealt with some pretty poor sanitation conditions. [*John Schehrer*]

Just west of the Big Chief Mine in Picher, Oklahoma, miner's shacks and shanties sprawl over the landscape, circa 1920. [John Schehrer]

Close-up of Main Street in Picher, Oklahoma. [John Schehrer]

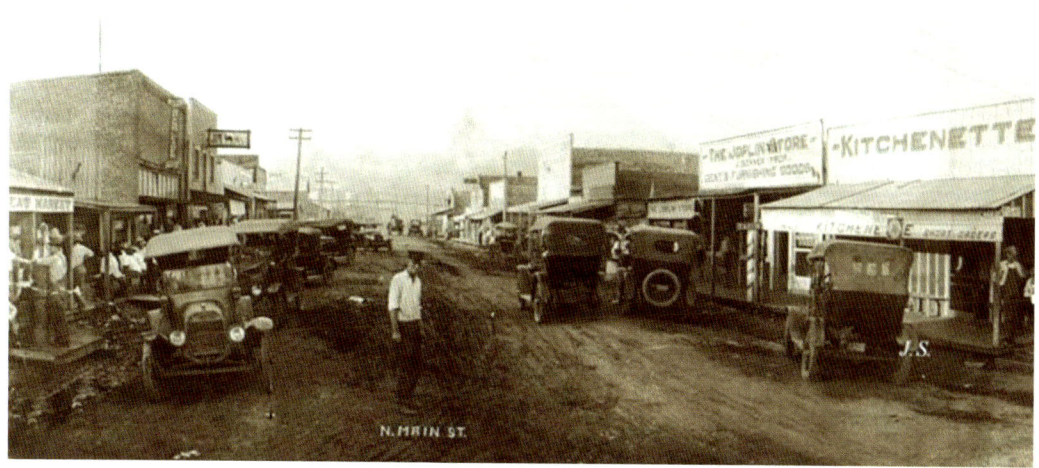

Main Street in Picher, Oklahoma, *circa* 1920. This would have been a familiar site to Lana's mother, Mildred, and if it followed the pattern of most mining towns of that era, she no doubt witnessed some interesting events going on in such a rough looking place. [*John Schehrer*]

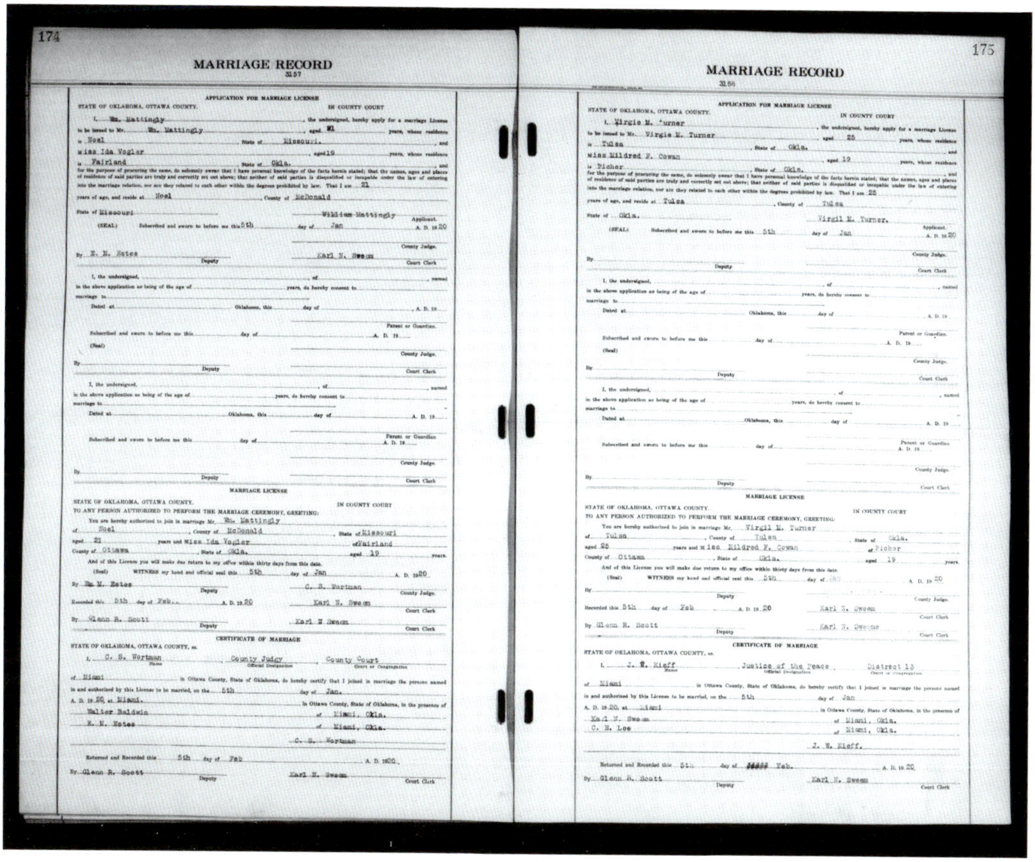

174

MARRIAGE RECORD

3157

APPLICATION FOR MARRIAGE LICENSE

STATE OF OKLAHOMA, OTTAWA COUNTY. IN COUNTY COURT

I, Wm. Mattingly, the undersigned, hereby apply for a marriage License to be issued to Mr. Wm. Mattingly, aged 21 years, whose residence is Noel, State of Missouri, and Miss Ida Vogler, aged 19 years, whose residence is Fairland, State of Okla., and for the purpose of procuring the same, do solemnly swear that I have personal knowledge of the facts herein stated; that the names, ages and places of residence of said parties are truly and correctly set out above; that neither of said parties is disqualified or incapable under the law of entering into the marriage relation, nor are they related to each other within the degrees prohibited by law. That I am 21 years of age, and reside at Noel, County of McDonald, State of Missouri

William Mattingly, Applicant.

(SEAL) Subscribed and sworn to before me this 5th day of Jan A. D. 1920

County Judge.

By E. M. Estes, Deputy — Karl N. Sweem, Court Clerk

I, the undersigned, ____ of ____, named in the above application as being of the age of ____ years, do hereby consent to marriage to ____

Dated at ____ Oklahoma, this ____ day of ____, A. D. 19__

Parent or Guardian.

Subscribed and sworn to before me this ____ day of ____ A. D. 19__

(Seal) County Judge.

By ____ Deputy — Court Clerk

I, the undersigned, ____ of ____, named in the above application as being of the age of ____ years, do hereby consent to marriage to ____

Dated at ____ Oklahoma, this ____ day of ____ A. D. 19__

Parent or Guardian

Subscribed and sworn to before me this ____ day of ____ A. D. 19__

County Judge.

By ____ Deputy — Court Clerk

MARRIAGE LICENSE

STATE OF OKLAHOMA, OTTAWA COUNTY. IN COUNTY COURT

TO ANY PERSON AUTHORIZED TO PERFORM THE MARRIAGE CEREMONY, GREETING:

You are hereby authorized to join in marriage Mr. Wm. Mattingly of Noel, County of McDonald, State of Missouri aged 21 years and Miss Ida Vogler of Fairland County of Ottawa, State of Okla. aged 19 years.

And of this License you will make due return to my office within thirty days from this date.

(Seal) WITNESS my hand and official seal this 5th day of Jan A. D. 1920

By Em M. Estes, Deputy — C. S. Wortman, County Judge.

Recorded this 5th day of Feb.. A. D. 1920 — Karl N. Sweem, Court Clerk

By Glenn R. Scott, Deputy — Karl N Sweem, Court Clerk

CERTIFICATE OF MARRIAGE

STATE OF OKLAHOMA, OTTAWA COUNTY, ss.

I, C. S. Wortman (Name), County Judgy (Official Designation), County Court (Court or Congregation) of Miami in Ottawa County, State of Oklahoma, do hereby certify that I joined in marriage the persons named in and authorized by this License to be married, on the 5th day of Jan. A. D. 1920, at Miami. in Ottawa County, State of Oklahoma, in the presence of

Walter Baldwin of Miami, Okla.

E. M. Estes of Miami, Okla.

C. S. Wortman

Returned and Recorded this 5th day of Feb A. D. 1920.

By Glenn R. Scott, Deputy — Karl N. Sweem, Court Clerk

175

MARRIAGE RECORD

3158

APPLICATION FOR MARRIAGE LICENSE

STATE OF OKLAHOMA, OTTAWA COUNTY. IN COUNTY COURT

I, Virgie M. Turner, the undersigned, hereby apply for a marriage License to be issued to Mr. Virgie M. Turner, aged 25 years, whose residence is Tulsa, State of Okla., and Miss Mildred F. Cowan, aged 19 years, whose residence is Picher, State of Okla., and for the purpose of procuring the same, do solemnly swear that I have personal knowledge of the facts herein stated; that the names, ages and places of residence of said parties are truly and correctly set out above; that neither of said parties is disqualified or incapable under the law of entering into the marriage relation, nor are they related to each other within the degrees prohibited by law. That I am 25 years of age, and reside at Tulsa, County of Tulsa, State of Okla.

Virgil M. Turner. Applicant.

(SEAL) Subscribed and sworn to before me this 5th day of Jan A. D. 1920

County Judge.

By ____ Deputy — Court Clerk

I, the undersigned, ____ of ____, named in the above application as being of the age of ____ years, do hereby consent to marriage to ____

Dated at ____ Oklahoma, this ____ day of ____ A. D. 19__

Parent or Guardian.

Subscribed and sworn to before me this ____ day of ____ A. D. 19__

(Seal) County Judge.

By ____ Deputy — Court Clerk

I, the undersigned, ____ of ____, named in the above application as being of the age of ____ years, do hereby consent to marriage to ____

Dated at ____ Oklahoma, this ____ day of ____ A. D. 19__

Parent or Guardian

Subscribed and sworn to before me this ____ day of ____ A. D. 19__

County Judge.

By ____ Deputy — Court Clerk

MARRIAGE LICENSE

STATE OF OKLAHOMA, OTTAWA COUNTY. IN COUNTY COURT

TO ANY PERSON AUTHORIZED TO PERFORM THE MARRIAGE CEREMONY, GREETING:

You are hereby authorized to join in marriage Mr. Virgil M. Turner of Tulsa, County of Tulsa, State of Okla. aged 25 years and Miss Mildred F. Cowan of Picher County of Ottawa, State of Okla. aged 19 years.

And of this License you will make due return to my office within thirty days from this date.

(Seal) WITNESS my hand and official seal this 5th day of [illegible] A. D. 1920

By ____ Deputy — County Judge.

Recorded this 5th day of Feb A. D. 1920 — Karl N. Sweem, Court Clerk

By Glenn R. Scott, Deputy — Karl N. Sweeme, Court Clerk

CERTIFICATE OF MARRIAGE

STATE OF OKLAHOMA, OTTAWA COUNTY, ss.

I, J. W. Kieff (Name), Justice of the Peace (Official Designation), District 13 (Court or Congregation) of Miami in Ottawa County, State of Oklahoma, do hereby certify that I joined in marriage the persons named in and authorized by this License to be married, on the 5th day of Jan A. D. 1920, at Miami in Ottawa County, State of Oklahoma, in the presence of

Karl N. Sweem of Miami, Okla.

C. E. Lee of Miami, Okla.

J. W. Kieff.

Returned and Recorded this 5th day of Feb. A. D. 1920.

By Glenn R. Scott, Deputy — Karl N. Sweem, Court Clerk

Marriage License of Lana's parents, John Virgil Madison Turner & Mildred Frances Cowan. [*Source Oklahoma, County Marriages, 1890-1995*]

2

Just Call Me Judy

Lana was the only child of John Virgil Madison Turner and Mildred Cowan. The Lana Turner everyone is familiar with was a creation of Hollywood. The real Lana was actually named Julia Jean Turner at the time of her birth. Later, after moving to California and being christened into the Catholic faith, she was given the additional names of Mildred Francis, making her full name Julia Jean Mildred Francis Turner. If you ask the people of Wallace, Idaho, they will tell you that Julia Jean also was not the real Lana. To them, she will always be remembered by her childhood nickname of just plain Judy, a curly headed little girl skipping, laughing and playing just like the other children in this Panhandle mining town.

As for when she was born, this, like many other areas of Lana's early life, is surrounded by controversy and mystery. Where was she born, and when? It is possible that she was actually conceived in Oklahoma, either in the mining town of Picher, or in the city of Tulsa. Maybe she was even born in Tulsa. Or was she conceived in Burke, Idaho, and born in Wallace? It is purported that Julia Jean Turner was born in Wallace, Idaho, on February 8, 1921, thirteen months after the marriage of her parents. Confusion seems to surround the exact date of her birth, with some claiming she was born in 1920. If this were the case, it means the fifteen-year-old Mildred was already very pregnant on her wedding day, with Lana being born one month later. This then leaves us with another question. Was she actually born in Wallace, Idaho? Or could she have been born in Oklahoma, or someplace in-between? Considering the extremely bad weather they would have encountered in a move from Oklahoma to Wallace, Idaho, I find it hard to believe that the heavily pregnant Mildred made that trip during the months of January or February. Lana states in her book: "I am one year younger than the records show. Now, if I were going to lie about my age, I might as well make it two, three, or five years." It's easy to guess why: to hide the fact that her mother was already pregnant with her when she got married. I am not saying this is what happened. I am only providing a possible explanation. On the flip side, the evidence seems to point more to a marriage of impulse. If Mildred had been pregnant, at fifteen years old, it is most likely that her father would have insisted on a shotgun wedding, negating the need for them to elope and lie about their ages on the marriage license. Until the birth record for Julia Jean Turner (Lana) becomes available in either the year 2020 or 2021, we are going to be left to wonder and speculate.

What we do know for sure is that at some time between their marriage in January 1920 and Julia/Lana's purported birth in 1921, the newlyweds John and Mildred Turner made their move from Tulsa, Oklahoma, to the cramped and booming town of Burke, located in North Idaho's Silver Valley. Although working in a Tulsa, Oklahoma, bakery at the time of their marriage, John may have felt that the need for lead and zinc miners in Burke would be a good financial move. Yet, I question the validity of this, as there were plenty of mines just a few miles away from Tulsa. Were they offering higher pay and better conditions in Burke? I've been told by a local historian that the mining companies in Burke were very family friendly, offering perks to married couples that helped with things like home ownership and medical care. Whatever the reasons, John and Mildred were starting their married life in a town fraught with disasters, both natural and man-made. Upon arrival, they could not have missed the rubble and debris left behind from the explosion of the Frisco Mill. In 1892, Burke gained notoriety for violent conflict and confrontation when striking Union miners ended up in a deadly gun battle with guards and non-Union replacement workers at the mill and mines. The Unionists had managed to obtain a box of black powder, which they sent down the hill and straight into a flume that went into the mine building, blowing up the Frisco Mill. Further violent encounters broke out in 1899, and this time the Bunker Hill mine was blown up with dynamite. If these violent encounters weren't enough trouble, Burke was also plagued with avalanches that caused so much damage, some of the smaller neighboring towns were completely wiped out. Fire was also a major concern, especially with so many wooden buildings cramped tightly together due to the lack of space. Somehow, I do not think that this rough town frightened or concerned either one of them, since both were already well acquainted with life in a mining town.

The couple took up residence in a small house on the same side of the mountain where the Star Mine sits. The house no longer exists, but the foundation is still there. It was in this home where Lana claims to have memories of her father holding her up on his shoulders to watch the train pass by their house. This has the ring of truth, since the tracks would indeed have gone right past their home. John likely took up employment in one of the many mines operating at the time, and, if Lana's personal account is correct, her mother was taken to Providence Hospital in Wallace, at the beginning of Burke Canyon, where Julia Jean Turner, the future Lana, was born. Nobody knows exactly for how long the family stayed in Burke before moving to neighboring Wallace, but if I had to guess, my money would be on the year 1923, after the big fire that swept through Burke and burned most of the town. I suspect their house was one of those caught up in the inferno.

The mining town of Burke, Idaho in 1891. When the newlyweds John and Mildred Turner arrived, it wouldn't have looked much different. Notice how narrow the road is, with the railroad tracks going through the center of town. The canyon where the town was built measured a mere 300 feet across.

An early postcard of Burke, Idaho.

Another early image of Burke, Idaho. Notice how the buildings on the left side are built right up against the surface of the mountain.

One of the few remaining original residences left in Burke, built sometime after the fire of 1923. The house sits vacant, but is owned by someone and is sign posted as private property.

A close-up of the door from the remaining residence in Burke.

The Morrow Retail Store in Burke, still standing right after the 1923 fire. [*Barnard Stockbridge Collection, University of Idaho, Special Collections and Archives*]

What remains of the Morrow Retail Store, as photographed by the author in 2019.

Another view of what is left of the Morrow Retail Store. It's hard to believe that at one time this was a bustling street, alive with families, shoppers and men off to the mines.

One more view of the Morrow Retail Store from a distance.

Another building that would have been a familiar sight to Lana's parents. This was originally the office for the Hercules Mine, and later was turned into a boarding house when the mine closed down. The author wanted to capture a feeling of age after she photographed and processed this shot.

Another shot of the Hercules Mine office from a slight distance.

A shot taken from the bottom of the hill that the old office sits on. It would be wonderful to see this grand old building restored, but being in a superfund site might make that difficult. This is also on private property, so please do not trespass.

An original photo from 1910 showing the Hercules Mine office in the forefront of the photo. It is located in a section of Burke known as Gorge Gulch.

Burke and the Hecla Star Mine as they look today. On October 14, 1891, the Hecla Mining Company was incorporated in the State of Idaho by founders Amasa Campbell, Patsy Clark and John Finch. The Star mine, which shut down in 1982, goes down in history as the deepest mine in North America, sinking 8,100 feet into the Earth.

Another view of the Hecla Star mining operation. The lush Idaho landscape brings a touch of surreal beauty to these abandoned buildings.

Standing as strong brick sentinels over the once bustling town.

The Star Mine sorting plant, covered passage and ore conveyors. Behind the sorting plant was the engineering building that included the electrical and welding rooms.

The Star Mine sorting plant in black and white.

The main offices of the Hecla Star mine. Even in their current desolate state, they retain a sense of solid impressiveness.

The passage and platform connecting the sorting plant to the engineering building.

A view of the Star office buildings from what was once the location of two businesses, identified on the 1927 Sanborn Fire Map as a drug store and the neighboring grocery and feed goods shop. The rock walls were constructed by masons imported in from Italy who used no mortar. These walls are as strong today as when they were first built.

What used to be a drug store and the neighboring grocery and feed goods shop.

Sharing a wall with the former drug store was the combination billiards hall and confectionery, at least that was their designation in 1927. Today, it looks like it has been converted into a garage of some sort.

Another view of the combination billiards hall and confectionery. Today, we wouldn't think of running these two businesses from the same building for fear of subjecting minor children to the goings on in a billiards hall. How things have changed over the past century.

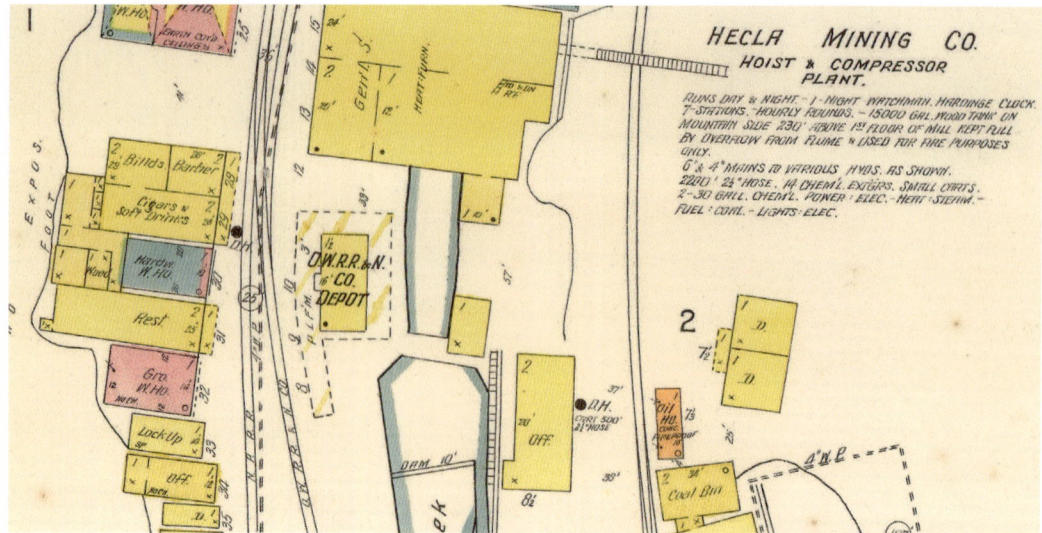

A blow-up of this business section from the 1918 Idaho Sanborn Fire Map for Burke. This is how it would have looked during the time Lana lived here with her parents, before the 1923 fire. [*Idaho Sanborn Fire Insurance Maps, University of Idaho, Special Collections and Archives*]

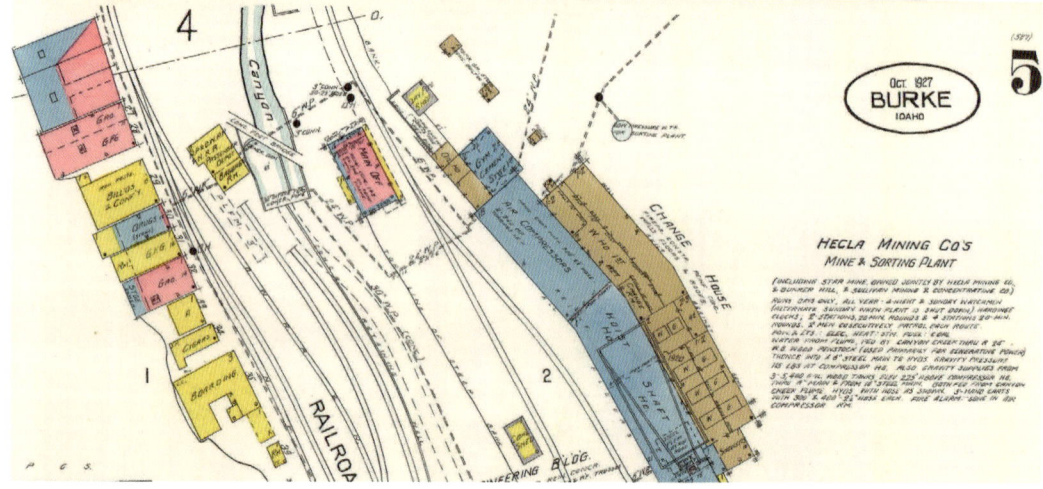

The same business section on the 1927 Sanborn Map showing the changes after the 1923 fire. These are the current foundations still existing. [*Idaho Sanborn Fire Insurance Maps, University of Idaho, Special Collections and Archives*]

Opposite page: Looking down the creek from Burke. It's hard to believe that an area full of so much natural beauty is considered contaminated.

A wider view looking down the creek, showing the lush greenery, majestic mountains and blue skies that this area of Idaho is famous for. It's truly breathtaking.

Providence Hospital in Wallace, Idaho, where it is claimed that Julia Jean Turner (Lana) was born in February 1921. Formerly located at the mouth of Burke Canyon, this magnificent building no longer exists. Founded by the Sisters of Providence in 1891, this hospital served this area of the Silver Valley area for seventy-seven years before closing in 1968. [*Barnard Stockbridge Collection, University of Idaho, Special Collections and Archives*]

3

In Her Footsteps

Some have written that due to leaving Wallace by the age of five or six years old, there are very few buildings that Lana could be directly connected with. I disagree. We know that her first public performance in front of an audience was at the Liberty Theater, and that her father performed regularly at the Elks Club. The home she lived in is still standing and listed on the National Historic Register, as is the Wallace Corner Store where her father worked for a time as a clerk. Although the Samuels Hotel, where it has been claimed her mother worked in a hair salon, no longer exists, the grounds still do in the form of a small public park. The location at Pearl and 7th Streets, where one of the few known photos was taken of her as a child, also still exists. But to say that these were the only places that she had any personal connection to is just ridiculous. Nearly the entire town of Wallace is a historic district. As a child, she would have window shopped with her parents, eyes wide with wonder at the colorful displays of clothing, toys and jars of hard candy. I can see her, face pressed against one of the old brick walls, eyes tightly closed, as she counted to twenty while her playmates found spots to tuck themselves into during a game of hide-and-seek. I know she also played tag with the neighborhood kids, as some of them regaled years ago in newspaper interviews about her life in Wallace. She would have walked hand-in-hand with her father as they headed to the Liberty Theater, no doubt her small fingers extended as she ran them along the cool surface of the buildings they passed. Certainly, she must have gone into a least a couple of the grocery stores, the bakery or to the butcher shop with her mother, savoring the smell of fresh food in a way that we cannot even fathom with the wrapped, canned and boxed products we buy today. I cannot believe that, like any other child, she did not press her little nose up against a few windows to see what was going on inside, her curious eyes seeking out the source of a sudden burst of laughter. She and her parents made friends, visited people in their homes, and shared the joy of parades and other public celebrations with the wider community. She has mentioned how she would save five cents of her lunch money every day so that she could afford the twenty-five cents to go to the Saturday matinee, which indicated that she may have attended school in Wallace for at least a few months before moving to California. Of course, that would only stand true if Wallace actually had a school lunch program at that time. In any case, her memory and the places she knew are alive and well in the town of Wallace and she left her own mark, even if in only the smallest of ways.

We can only speculate about the causes that led to the family leaving Burke and settling in Wallace. Maybe John Virgil Turner saw it as an opportunity to get out of the mines, hoping for a new way to support his family in a less dangerous profession. Although we have not found any actual evidence of it, Lana has said that when her family moved to Wallace, her father went into partnership with another man to open a laundry. Some earlier Wallace residents believe that he only worked in a laundry, and according to Wallace District Mining Museum, he worked at the City Dye Works dry cleaning company. According to the *Wallace Miner* newspaper, in multiple editions in 1907, the dry cleaners was located at 411 Cedar Street, where the post office is now located. What we do know for sure is that he worked at the Wallace Corner Company in 1924/25, according to page 69 of the Wallace City Directory, which reads: "Turner John V (Mildred), clerk, Wallace Corner Company, home, 217 Bank." Interesting to note is that when the family moved into the home at 217 Bank Street, it was also being operated as a bakery, an occupation that John had been employed at in Tulsa, Oklahoma.

Unfortunately for the family, John had a fondness for gambling, drinking and, so some have said, visiting the Red Light district of Wallace. Lana herself has stated that her father would often resort to gambling when the family funds were running low, but it wasn't clarified if this was because he was out of work or just liked to gamble for extra money. Either way, I'm sure gambling with the family's rent and grocery money must have caused some stress and consternation in the home. As for visiting the Red Light ladies, that would not have been uncommon or unexpected in Wallace. Little Julia Jean/Judy/Lana probably came across a few of these ladies on a regular basis, and may have accepted a candy or two from them. This was all part and parcel of the world she lived in. For a short period, the family lived at the Pacific Hotel, which was located near 800 Bank & 7th streets, where the Shoshone County Public Safety Facility is currently located.

Above left: This image is purported to be of Julia Jean (Lana) Turner and her parents, Mildred and John. She appears to be about two or three years old and it was most likely taken in Burke, Idaho. The original of this image has turned brown and brittle with age and is in a private collection. I have been asked to not reveal the name of the collector, other than to say that this photo was given to their relative by Lana personally many, many years ago in Hollywood as part of a collection she was compiling.

Above right: A blow-up of the child purported to be Julia Jean (Lana) in the family group photo.

Julia Jean (Lana) walking up 7th Street in Wallace, at about five years of age. This image, used many times in articles, books and blogs, appears to be in the public domain. Attempts to find any information on who owns the original have turned up no results. Lana's daughter, Cheryl Crane, has stated that she doesn't have any early photos of her mother.

A photograph looking down 7th Street in Wallace, Idaho, taken by the author, with a superimposition of the Julia Jean (Lana) photo taken in this same location *circa* 1926.

A photo of the entire section of 7th Street, facing Bank Street. The large building behind Lana's right shoulder is the Idaho Press Building. The building closest to her right shoulder, with the awning, is a private residence. The awning is no longer on the house.

Now the Wallace Corner Hotel Espresso Bar, during the time the Turner family lived here, father John was employed at this building as a clerk when it was the Wallace Corner Company in 1924. I believe that at one time this was known as the Fuller Building.

A front view of the Wallace Corner Hotel. The National Register of Historic Places describes the building: "The Fuller Hotel is a three-story brick block which has been hideously stuccoed. Built in 1890, it was the finest hotel and largest building in Wallace for its time."

The Wallace Corner Hotel from in front of the Tabor building. The wrap-around balcony is a new addition to the building and is not original.

The underside of the wrap-around balcony.

On left side of image, just past the Grand, you can see the Liberty Theater, located in the FOE building, where it has been claimed Lana performed for the first time as a small child. A few buildings down from that, also on the left, is the Wallace Corner Company building where her father worked. If you look down the right side, all the way down, the large building with the steel triangular structure on the roof was the Samuel's Hotel, where it is purported her mother worked at a hair salon.

The Fraternal Order of Eagles (FOE) building, which used to house the Liberty Theater. Next to it is the J. Furst building.

Another view of the FOE building, now operating as the Dayrock Bar. If you visit Wallace, stop in for some craft beer and live music.

A closer view of the J. Furst building, constructed in 1900.

The side of the J. Furst building offers us a fascinating glimpse of ghost signs painted on the brick. In 1904, this was Fahle's Hotel, as you can see from the original words still visible after all these years. Also, just barely readable is an advertisement for Gilt Top Beer.

The view looking down Cedar Street. Julia Jean (Lana) would have gone down this street often as a child.

Another view of the ghost signs on the J. Furst building.

Above left: This Powers Excelite Cameragraph Projector is very much like the one that would have played movies at the Liberty Theater when Julia Jean (Lana) was going there as a child. This particular one is in the basement of the Oasis Museum just down the street, across from the Tabor building.

Above right: A close-up showing details of the Powers Excelite.

Another view of the Powers Excelite in the Oasis Museum.

This small community park was once the site of the Samuel's Hotel where Lana's mother was employed. The Hale building is in the background.

The Smokehouse, or the Delasmutt Block as it is officially registered, was built in 1890 and has been in continual use since then. It was originally the first County Courthouse in Wallace. This was just a six-minute walk away from Lana's home and since the area was a main shopping district, she no doubt passed the building frequently.

The Ryan Hotel, opened in 1903, located on Cedar street between 6th and 7th, is one of Wallace's longest operating hotels. They offer a massage room that is equipped with a claw-foot soaking tub.

Another view of the Ryan Hotel and the neighboring Barnard building.

Winter along Bank Street in Wallace. Prominently visible at the corner of Bank and 6th Streets is the Rossi Insurance building with its distinctive pressed metal blue turret. Also in front of this building you will find yourself standing at the Center of the Universe, with a fancy manhole cover marking the spot. Is it really the Center of the Universe? As many in Wallace would say: prove it isn't!

Same view of Bank Street in the summer.

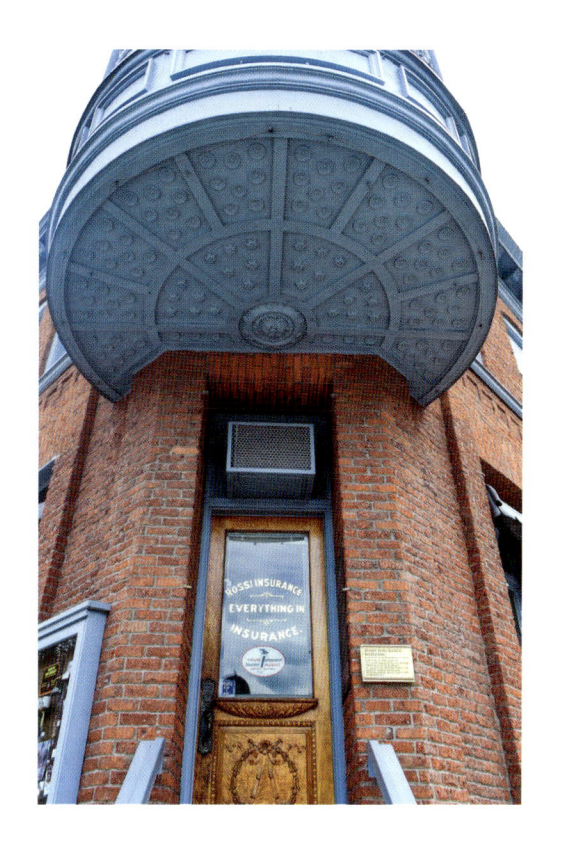

Clockwise from top left:

Looking up at the pressed metal turret of the Rossi Insurance building. I wonder if young Lana ever stood in this exact same spot and counted the stars and medallions?

The Rossi turret from the side.

Entrance to the Rossi Insurance building. Even the carved door is a work of art.

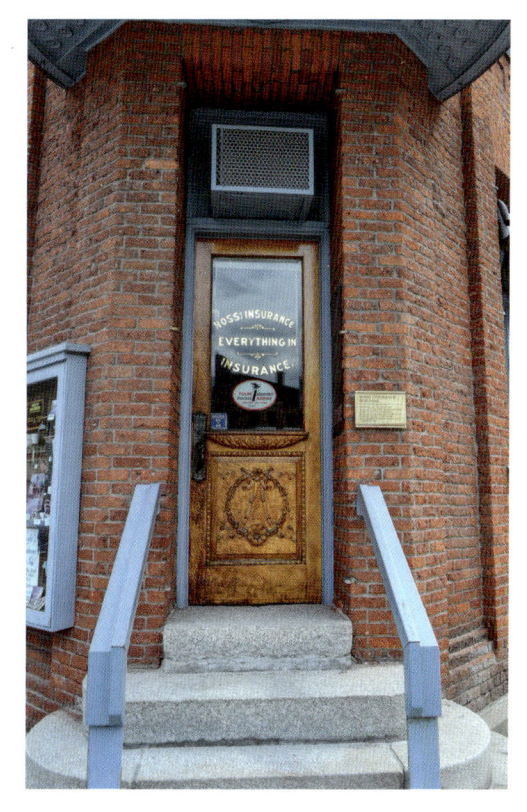

Counterclockwise from left:

Original decorative details are still visible on the Queen Anne style Rossi building.

The Center of the Universe, at least according to Wallace residents.

One of the 100+ year old stairways that Wallace is famous for. Where does it lead? You'll have to climb it to find out, but be prepared because it is quite a workout! Some of these stairways are over 100 feet long.

Albi's Gem Bar was at one time one of Wallace's famous steakhouses.

Sweet's Hotel and the Jameson Inn are located behind the Wallace Corner Hotel where Lana's father used to work. Both were built in the late 1890s. It is claimed that Room 1 at the Jameson is haunted by a woman named Maggie who used to come to Wallace from St. Louis for a few months every year until she suddenly stopped coming. Rumor was that she had been killed in some sort of train accident in St. Louis. At the time, Maggie was staying at the Jameson Hotel. Room 1 was originally Room 3. I found it interesting when I came across a small advertisement placed in the *Wallace Miner* newspaper, dated October 3, 1912. It reads: "Position Wanted. A girl wants work with private family, restaurant or hotel. Inquire at Room 3, Jameson Block, city." Could this have been Maggie in Room 3?

The Northern Pacific Depot Museum in Wallace. Built in 1902, the depot had to be moved 200 feet from its original location in 1986 when the I-90 was being built and the depot was in its path.

Inside the Depot Museum..

The Oasis Bordello Museum, probably originally called "The Club Rooms" during the time the Turner family lived here. Downstairs was the bar and gambling areas, while upstairs was the brothel. In 1988, this brothel shut down permanently overnight when there were fears of an FBA raid about to happen. Today, the museum maintains the rooms exactly as they were when the ladies took off for safer pastures, leaving behind many personal items. Arcadia Publishing and The History Press have published a book called *Selling Sex in the Silver Valley* by local author Dr. Heather Branstetter, an interesting read about the story of prostitution in Wallace.

A close-up of the Oasis sign backdropped by beautiful blue skies.

The Arment was another brothel operating in Wallace during the time the Turners lived here. It shut its doors in 1977. It is now the Lux rooms.

Old stairs leading to the Lux Rooms brothel. Just imagine all the stories these stairs could tell!

The corner of Cedar and 6th Streets, with the Lucky Horseshoe and the Silver Corner Bar. The Arment building is located between them.

This was one of three livery stables that existed at one time in Wallace.

The backs of the Oasis and Arment brothels. Notice the enclosed staircase on the back of the Arment, which was intended to provide some privacy to visiting male clients.

The backs of a couple of other former brothels.

A front view of Sweet's Hotel. Some of the women who worked in the brothels often lived here in rented rooms.

Tabor's Emporium at Cedar and 6th Streets. This building was erected in 1933, after the original buildings were destroyed by a fire.

A view down one of the many alleys in Wallace. No doubt Julia Jean/Lana played in or walked down a few of them during her years in Wallace.

Along Bank Street, near the popular Wallace Brewing Company.

The Coeur d'Alene Hardware Company has been operating here since before 1890, making it the first mining supply company in the area to sell hardware and metal to miners and mining companies.

A wider view of the south side of Bank Street.

Another view of the Smokehouse.

Built in 1916, the First National Bank is a white terracotta Second Renaissance Revival building, with Doric columns, pediment entry, round-arched windows, cornice and parapet.

58

An upwards view of the First National Bank along the side wall.

The Gearon building, constructed in 1927.

A side view of the First National Bank and the Masonic Temple, now The Cobblestone.

An upwards view of the Masonic Temple from the doorway.

A perspective view of the Masonic Temple and First National Bank, showing the fine decorative details on both buildings.

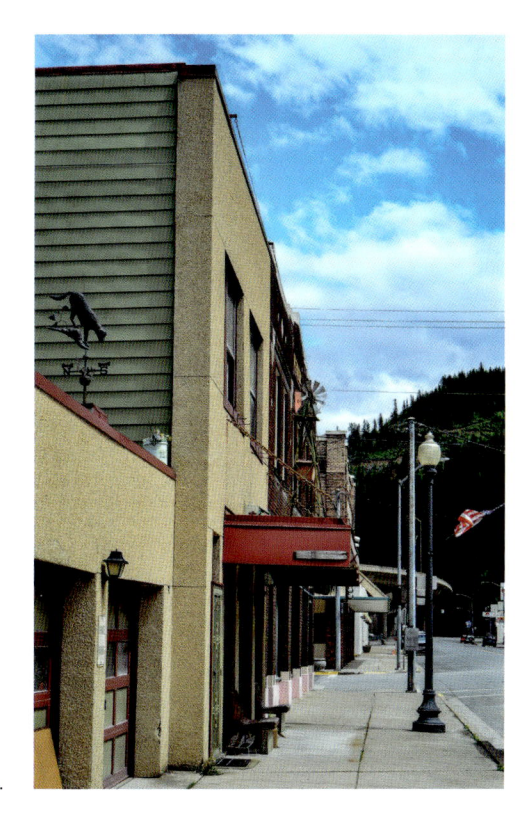

The north side of Bank Street, facing east.

Doorway of 613 Bank Street. At one time, this was the Rocky Mountain Telephone Building.

The Wallace City Hall, built in 1924. No doubt Julia Jean/Lana saw the actual construction going on, since it was right down the street from where her father worked, and across from the Samuel's Hotel, where it was claimed her mother worked.

The old Wallace Printing Company, established in 1906. This building is now listed for sale.

I'm not sure what was originally operated from here. It is now the Idaho Press Gallery.

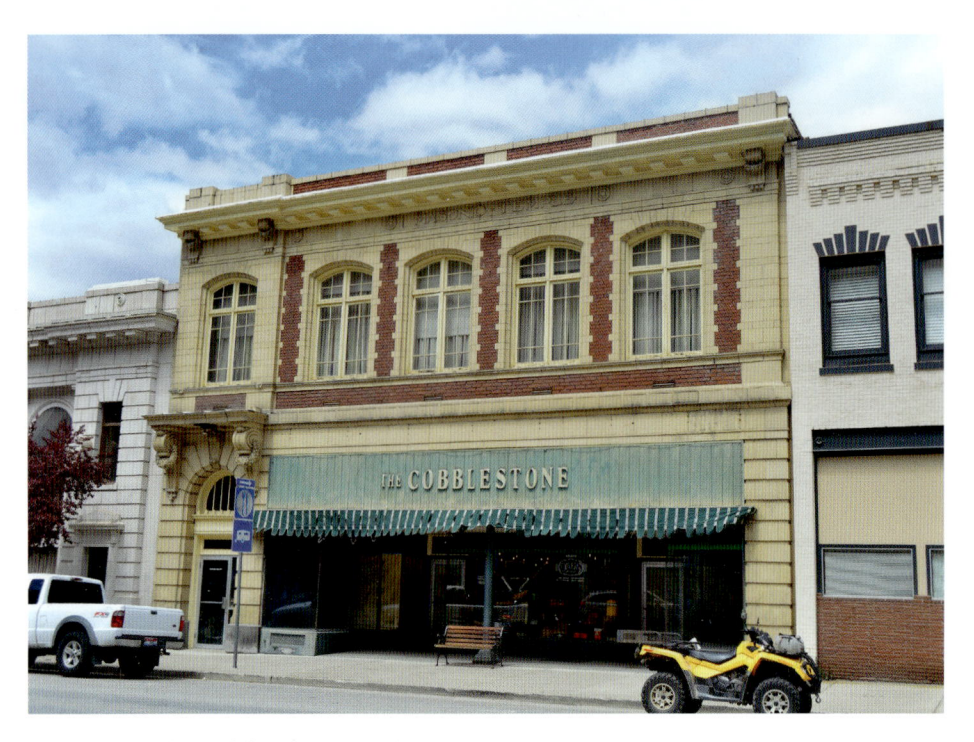

Full view of the beautiful Masonic Temple.

The corner of Bank and 7th Streets.

The Shoshone County Courthouse, built in 1905, is a three-story building of the Neo-classical Revival style. The concrete blocks were made from ore tailings.

Benevolent and Protective Order of Elks (B.P.O.E.) building, constructed in 1924, where Juila Jean/Lana's father often performed his tap-dancing routines. This is also where her mother participated in a fashion show, and little Julia, wishing to be like her mother, donned a fur jacket and took to the stage. Apparently, the audience loved this impromptu performance by the cheeky four-year-old Julia/Lana.

Built in 1916 for Julius Cohn, the Shoshone building still retains its poly-chromatic decorative detailing. I was given the privilege by the current owners to photograph the original interior on the second floor. This truly is an amazing piece of Wallace history. The EurekaSally Gallery of Art & Chocolate is located on the ground floor and she sells some fantastic all-natural, homemade dark chocolate.

Even the alleys in Wallace offer interesting views and perspectives. Those stairways you see were more often than not used as back entrances to a brothel or to the rooms of one of the working girls.

The Hall Hotel, across from the Smokehouse.

One of the charming trolleys operating in Wallace.

A wander through the back alleys of Wallace often reveals unexpected surprises, like this vintage Army vehicle behind the Shoshone Building.

An old metal staircase located down one of the many alleys in Wallace. At one time, many of these stairs were used by men to secretly enter the private room of one of the local prostitutes.

A winter scene in Wallace. Not much changed from when a young Lana wandered these streets.

Another wintery street in Wallace.

4

217 Bank Street—A Brief History

Lana recalled many happy memories of singing, dancing and listening to music in this house on Bank Street. It would be very easy to assume, considering what was to follow once the family left their cozy little home in Wallace for the wild San Francisco streets, that Julia Jean Turner lived her happiest and most secure years in the Silver Valley, when her parents were still together and life wasn't a series of one foster home after another. First, let's get the misconceptions out of the way. I've read too many articles where the writer has stated categorically that the family lived on the second floor of the house. Possible? Yes. But we do not know for sure. During the time the Turner family resided here, the home was also occupied by Fred and Mable Viele. At one time a bakery had been operated from the front ground-floor section. A section of the ground floor had been divided off at the back into a small apartment, and this is where the Turner family may have lived.

The house was built sometime between 1905 and 1910. The 1910 Federal Census has the address listed as 217 Bank with William H. Downs, a single man, as head-of-house, and states he was a baker. However, also at the same address listed as a head-of-house was Thomas Peterson, and his employment was also a baker. Enumerated with Thomas Peterson were his wife Caroline Peterson, and their widowed daughter, Elma Lenard, and her child, Rae. This census year does not tell us who owned the house. This must have been a busy and very cramped house and bakery business in 1910, as we also see that at 215 Bank Street lived Hanna Brown, a widow, with her two sons, Thomas and Foster. The thing is, 215 was not actually a separate house. This was the back-portion apartment on the ground floor, but was given a different address from the main house of 217 Bank. It is possible that since William Downs was a single man, he slept on a cot in the bakery, which seems very possible when ten years later we look at the 1920 census.

We see that by 1920, Thomas Peterson and wife Caroline are still living here, and this time, it tells us that he owned the house, so William Downs was probably an employee in the bakery.

Also living in the house are Fred Viele with wife, Mable Cora Bean, and daughters, Irene, Mable and Mary. The address of 215 Bank is no longer used, but it does state that Thomas and Caroline Peterson live in the back of the house and they are no longer running a bakery. Fred was working as an engineer with the railroad, while daughters Irene and Mable were employed at the theater as cashiers. Although which theater is not specified, we have clues that indicate it was the Liberty, where Julia/Lana first performed.

But what about William Downs? Well, on January 3, 1914, he married fellow lodger, Hanna Brown, in Wallace. They moved to Mullan, Idaho, before 1920 where, in 1921, he built a public garage.

Shortly after the 1920 census, Thomas and Caroline Peterson left Wallace, but we do not know if they continued to own the house and rent it out, or if they sold it to Fred Viele.

Thanks to Donna MacDonald, a great-great granddaughter of Fred and Mable Cora Viele, we know for a fact that the Turner family lived at the address with them as tenants. Donna, who lives in Texas and has never been to Idaho, grew up with stories from her grandfather Russel Clark's widow, Mary Wathen Clark, about Lana Turner living in the same house with his grandparents Fred and Mable Cora Viele. His mother, Irene Viele Clark, played piano for Lana's dance lessons, which may have taken place in Irene's rented accommodations at 509 First Street, where she lived with husband, Reed Clark, and son, Russel. The family of John Waurnis also rented the other section of this house.

Charles Seraphine is listed as head of house in the 1930 census, enumerated with son, Austin, and daughter, Agnes. Austin was running a butcher shop from here in 1930. By this time, Fred Viele had moved his family to 118 River Street. In 1935, Austin was living in Washington with his new wife, but returned to this house by 1940, where he continued his butcher shop. He may have returned to the house since his father was now residing in the Miner's Home in Wallace. In 1930, the family of Carl Anderson, his wife, Daisy, daughter, Mary, and son, Carl, Jr., lived in the rear addition of the house. Both families were renting.

So, we have now established that stories about the house having been either a bakery or a butcher shop are both correct. The Turners could have lived on either the top or ground floor, but we are not sure which. It is also very possible that the top floor was divided into two apartments at one time.

217 Bank Street as it looks today. There are two entry doors, one of which is on the far right. This one led to the stairs to the top floor, while the door on the left entered into the shop area and most likely to the living quarters at the back of the ground floor.

The upper floor of the house, with living quarters that may have been divided into two apartments.

A view of the 217 Bank Street house from Upper Bank Street.

A closer view of the house from Upper Bank Street.

The front porch of the house, where little Julia Jean/Lana Turner probably played as a child.

A closer view of the front porch. You can see that the doors and windows are original.

Clockwise from top left:

The front door from the porch leading to the upper floor stairs. Do doubt Julia Jean/Lana turned that exact doorknob, which is original to the door.

Inside shot of the ground floor front door that led into the bakery/butcher shop area, and probably to the back apartment.

The stairs leading to the upstairs living quarters. Did Julia Jean/Lana skip and dance up and down these stairs? Most likely. They would have been perfect for her father to teach her those tap dance routines.

Looking down the stairs to the front door entrance.

Inside the Julia Jean/Lana Turner home. The floorboards are original, the same ones she would have walked and danced on. I didn't take too many interior photos, just a few to share a peek in. The house is currently in the process of being repaired and restored by the owner, so there are a lot of construction and paint supplies inside.

A view through the upper floor windows, covered with lace panels, giving us a charming glimpse of how they may have looked when the Turner family lived here.

Pulling back the lace panel gives us a colorful view of rooftops back-dropped by lush green trees, exactly as Julia Jean/Lana would have seen them through her little girl eyes. This must have been a magical view to a young child.

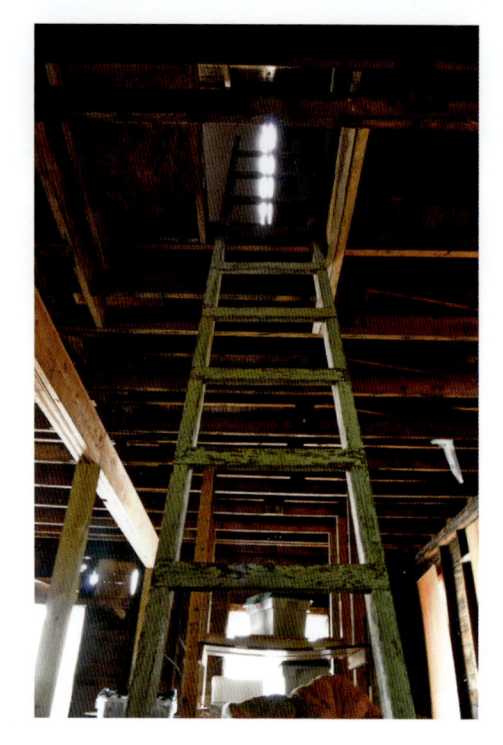

Ladder leading from the upper floor to the roof. Yes, this author did climb up, shaking like a nervous chihuahua the entire way up. Not the smartest thing to do with a leg muscle disability, but the author thought it was well worth it for the view.

View from the rooftop. Did little Julia Jean/Lana come up here to look at the stars with her father? She just might have.

Looking towards the main town from the rooftop. What a glorious view!

The upper level porch, where maybe the Turner family gathered on a hot summer night to catch a cool breeze.

Was this an original combination cabinet/shelf from the time the Turners lived here? I'm not sure, but it looks old and solid enough to have been.

The view that little Julia Jean/Lana would have seen from the front porch, looking across Bank Street.

— 2 —

France during World War One, was injured and received a Purple Heart. After the war he was a miner in Wallace. Irene was the manager of the State liquor store. She played the piano at the theater showing silent movies. Russ used to sit there and cry because he wanted to go home to bed. She also played the piano for Lana Turner's (the movie star later) dance lessons. Since both of his parents worked he was alone a lot and learned to cook for himself when he could barely see over the stove. He and his parents were Catholic and Russ was an altar boy. Later on he was a delivery boy for the town grocery. His biggest tips came from the prostitutes. During Russ's young years there

The letter written by Mary (Wathen) Clark, widow of Russel Clark. She is talking about how Russel's mother, Irene (Viele) Clark, managed the State Liquor Store, played the piano at the silent movies in the theater and how she also played piano during Julia Jean/Lana's dance lessons. We are not sure of where these dance lessons were conducted, whether at the Turner family home at 217 Bank Street, Irene's home at 25 Bank Street or at the Liberty Theater. Irene was a daughter of Fred and Mabel Cora (Bean) Viele. [*Donna MacDonald of Texas, from her personal family archive collection. Letter written by Mary Wathen Clark, widow of Donna MacDonald's grandfather Russel Clark*]

Photo is of Irene (Viele) Clark and younger sister Mabel (Viele) "Billie" Hoopengardner. On the back of the photo Irene has written "Billie and me." Photo *circa* 1916, which can be dated based on both girls having the popular "Castle Bob" hairstyle. Irene would have been nineteen years old, and Mabel would have been thirteen. [Donna MacDonald]

Fred Viele and daughter, Irene. Notice the wooden plank walkways between and in front of the houses. According to the 1909 edition of the *Machinists' Monthly Journal*, Volume 21, Fred was foreman at the roundhouse in Wallace. The Idaho Northern Railway was built from Enaville to Murray in 1910 by E. P. Spaulding. The president was Barney O'Neil, with Fred Viele as master mechanic. They operated a passenger train that was called the "Merry Widow," because of the wide smokestack on the engine. This railroad was washed out by the flood in 1917 and was never rebuilt. [Donna MacDonald]

Irene with youngest sister, Mary Isabel Viele. It's hard to tell for sure, but this might be a photo taken on the top floor porch of the 217 Bank Street house, where the original door and windows have been replaced with modern ones. Mary looks about twelve years old, the age she was when the family moved here about 1920. The door in this image is very much like the ones on the ground floor of the 217 Bank Street house. [*Donna MacDonald*]

Fred Viele and daughter Mary Isabel, taken New Year's Day, 1919. [*Donna MacDonald*]

The three Viele sisters, Irene, Mary and Mabel. It looks like Placer Creek is flowing past in the background. [*Donna MacDonald*]

Mabel Cora (Bean) Viele, who went by the nickname "Biele." [*Donna MacDonald*]

5

The San Francisco Years

Although the focus of this book was on Lana Turner's early childhood in Wallace, I felt it would be of interest to at least include her first three years in California, up to age nine. So many rumors about her early life have been twisted and not properly researched that places, time frames and events have become intertwined into a ball of confusion. This section serves to put these rumors to rest with facts. First, Mildred and Lana did not leave John behind in Wallace and run away to California, as some writers have claimed. The family left together. Lana seems confused when it comes to the story about her father's involvement in making bootleg liquor. One account has the family suddenly leaving Wallace because he was caught by the law making bootleg liquor, while in another account she claims that during their short time in Stockton, CA, she overheard her parents arguing in the basement and heard the word "bootlegging." Later, she bragged to a playmate that her father was a bootlegger when she wanted to one-up the girl while talking about what their fathers did for a living. The little girl supposedly told her father, who then called the law. I am doubtful that he was chased out of Wallace for bootlegging. During that time, Wallace law enforcement were turning a blind eye to bathtub stills and other illicit alcohol coming into the area from Montana.

The Stockton story would be the more likely of the two. It is more probable that the family left Wallace because John was deep in debt from gambling. Life did not go well for the Turners when they arrived in the Golden State. From what can be gathered, their first few months were spent living as vagabonds around the Stockton and Daly City areas. Once the family finally found lodgings in San Francisco, the marriage of John and Mildred was soon on the rocks, leading to separation. John went his way, Mildred went hers, and Julia Jean/Lana found herself being shuffled from one foster home to another. Lana offered the explanation that her mother could not afford to pay for housing for the both of them, so her mother placed her with other families. This simply does not make sense, as placing Lana in foster homes would also have cost her mother room and board for the child. This was the era of the Great Depression and people could not afford to feed and house the children of others for free. The truth is that both parents were using aliases while working in less than savory occupations or involved in illegal activities. John Virgil Turner has been described as a gambler, a con man, a bootlegger, a boozer and a womanizer, but as it turns out, her mother Mildred was also employed in what was considered a less than respectable occupation. Contrary to what Lana was always led to believe, her mother was not working in a hair salon or as a laundress. In actuality, she had dyed her hair and was working in a night club. When reporting John Turner's death, the *San Francisco Chronicle* would describe her as a blonde night club entertainer. The address given as her place of residence was located in the infamous Tenderloin District of San Francisco, notorious for its gambling dens, speakeasies, drugs, crime, prostitution and tawdry night clubs. This is why she could not have young Lana living with her. It would have interfered with her late-night working hours, and most housing in that area was set up for single people or couples without children. Since Mildred does not appear in the census for 1930, I am convinced that, like her estranged husband, she was using an assumed name.

Lana always told people that on the night of her father's death she was living with the family of Clarence, Julia and Beverly Hislop in Stockton, CA. A newspaper report at the time of her father's death states that she was living with a Mrs. Virginia Britt in Stockton, and not with the Hislop family. The Hislop family lived at 1727 McKinley, Stockton. Living near the Hislops were John & Ethel Britt, who had a married daughter named Virginia Cary. This is probably who the newspaper was referring to. Curiously enough, Julia Jean/Lana also does not appear anywhere in the 1930 Census. Not with her mother, father or any of the known foster families it was claimed she was living with. It is my belief that she also was given an assumed name and placed with a family in the Stockton, San Jose or Lodi areas.

Lana's father was beaten to death after a craps game in San Francisco on December 14, 1930. His killer was never found. It was claimed that he often had to change his name when he owed gambling debts or was involved in bootlegging or some con scheme.

Virgil does show up in the 1930 census, living at the Hotel Irwin on 108 Fourth Street, under the name of Ernest Johnson, the alias that was reported in the news account of his death. He shaved four years from his actual age, and said that his father was born in the Irish Free State and his mother in Holland. The only truthful statements he provides are that he was born in Tennessee and was working as an insurance salesman at that time. This job didn't last long and at the time of his death he was working as a longshoreman.

The *San Francisco Chronicle*, December 15, 1930, reported his death on page 6:

BLOW KILLS VETERAN IN MYSTERY ROW
Body Found in Potrero With Watch, Pin and Money Missing
With all the appearances of having been "taken for a ride," the body of Virgil M. Turner, war veteran and stevedore boss, husband of a night club entertainer, was found yesterday morning in the Potrero district, behind the Southern Pacific roundhouse.

The body was propped in a sitting position against a warehouse at Mariposa and Minnesota streets. Other than a bruised eye, there were no signs of injury. Death was due to the blow on the eye.

GAMBLING ROW SUSPECTED

Police were inclined to a theory that Turner, sometimes known as (Ernie) Johnson, was killed in a gambling row in a down town alley, but the possibility that he was slain by gangsters also was under investigation.

Mrs. Mildred Turner, blonde night club entertainer, reported she had last seen her husband about 12:30 o'clock yesterday morning, and that he had been wearing a valuable diamond stickpin, carried a watch and considerable money. No money, watch or pin was found on the man.

CALLED ON WIFE

Turner, in company with a friend whose name has not been learned, visited the night club to talk with his wife, from whom he had been separated about a year.

He apparently returned to his hotel at Fourth and Mission streets in his coupe, and went out again about 2 o'clock in the morning. Who his companions were, if any, had not been learned early last night.

A daughter of Turner and his wife is Julia Jean Turner, 8, residing with Mrs. Virginia Britt at Stockton.

Death was caused by a cerebral hemorrhage, caused by the eye blow, autopsy revealed.

The *San Francisco Examiner*, also dated December 15, 1930, reported:

ENIGMA DEATH VICTIM FOUND

San Francisco police were given a baffling murder mystery to solve yesterday, when the body of Virgil M. Turner, 38, longshore foreman, was discovered huddled against a warehouse wall at Mariposa and Minnesota streets.

The only mark on Turner's body was a bruised eye. An autopsy showed he had died of a cerebral hemorrhage, probably caused by the blow that bruised his face. His wallet was found in a pocket of his overcoat, empty. There were no valuables on the body.

Turner lived under the name of "Ernie Johnson" at the Hotel Irwin, 108 Fourth Street. At the hotel it was said he had left his room about 6 o'clock without revealing where he intended going.

Turner has been estranged from his wife, Mildred, to whom he had been married for 11 years. They previously lived at Daly City. Mrs. Turner now lives at 760 Geary street. She appeared at the morgue to identify her husband's body, and told police she had talked with him at 5 o'clock Saturday night. The widow was prostrated at learning of Turner's death.

After the death of her father, Lana was placed with an Italian family in Lodi. She believed that her mother was employed in a beauty parlor owned by a woman named Chila Meadows, who about three months later invited Mildred and Lana to live with her. They moved into the apartment of the Meadows family, which included Chila's children, Hazel and George. Chila was actually Lucille Meadows, born in Guatemala, and married to Norman Leslie Meadows, a British immigrant to the United States who was employed as an assistant steward working on steamships. A news announcement shows us that Mr. Meadows died unexpectedly in New York on January 23, 1931. Lucille did not own a beauty parlor. She was the manager of the Greenwood Apartments at 1045 Post Street, where she also resided. The year of Mr. Meadows' death coincides with the time frame that Lana claims she and her mother took up residence with Lucille.

I find it interesting that in 1933 Mildred decided to move herself and Lana to Los Angeles. This was the same year that Prohibition ended in San Francisco, causing hundreds of speakeasies and night clubs to close shop in the Tenderloin.

3027

AUTOPSY SURGEON'S REPORT

San Francisco Dec 14, 1930

I hereby certify that I have performed an autopsy or made an examination upon the body of Virgil M. Turner at 1 P. M. 9,
and that the apparent cause of death is

Cerebral Hemorrhage
(Traumatic)

A. Berger Autopsy Surgeon.

Cause of death determined at inquest _____

The following organs have been forwarded by the Autopsy Surgeon to the **Coroner's Toxicologist** for examination:

Gastro intestinal tract _____ Other organs _____
Blood _____
Date _____ Time _____ Messenger _____
Written report on above received from Toxicologist _____ Date _____
Organs submitted to Pathologist for examination _____
Written report on above received and filed. Date _____

EVIDENCE

The following evidence _____ submitted to _____
for examination: _____
_____ Deputy.
Other evidence held at Coroner's office _____

Disposition _____ Date _____
Date of Inquest December 29th 1930
Verdict of Jury: That said deceased met his death at the hands of party or parties unknown to the jury.

PROPERTY

Property received by Deputy A. Trabucco
Clothes in Locker No. on hanger in locker #105
Cash—Currency No Gold No Silver No TOTAL No
Jewelry J. M. Ring, American Legion Emblem

Will No Bank book No
Discharge papers Yes Other effects memo book.
papers, cards, knife, pencil, cigarette lighter
Wallet, Pawn ticket #57637 Reliable Loan Office
Letter.

The above property checked and received by _____ Custodian of Property.
Time _____ Date _____

DISPOSITION OF PROPERTY

Received the above listed property:
Name Mrs. Mildred Turner.
Address 760 Geary St. #710 -
Relationship Wife.
Date _____ Deputy _____
Listing of Clothing—Page _____ Clothing book.

RECEIPT FOR CLOTHING

Name _____
Address _____
Relationship _____
Date _____ Deputy _____
Paste cancelled check here.

Autopsy Surgeon's Report for John Virgil Turner. [*San Francisco County Records, 1824-1997*]

Coroner's Report for John Virgil Turner. Witness Stanley Hergott, the Southern Pacific employee who found John Virgil Turner's body, would also be notified later that morning of the death of his mother. [*San Francisco County Records*]

Funeral Home Bill for John Virgil Turner. [*San Francisco Area Funeral Home Records, 1895-1985*]

Interment Record for John Virgil Turner. [*Ancestry.com. U.S. National Cemetery Interment Control Forms, 1928-1962*]

Want More? Videos Tours

I hope you have enjoyed this journey through the early beginnings of the life of Lana Turner. While doing my research, I often come across interesting websites or videos that I would like to share with readers. I feel that it brings the story to life even more, providing deeper insights and leading down other paths to explore. If you are so inclined, you might want to visit the following:

"Abandoned Cardin Oklahoma Drive" takes us on a journey down what was once the main street of Tar River/Cardin, Oklahoma. https://youtu.be/DvYaRMM5LiA

Also, by the same videographer above, "Most Toxic Place in America, Picher, Oklahoma." His video offers an amazing view of this abandoned town. https://youtu.be/1iBosc6rCFc

"Picher, the Town Oklahoma Forgot" is an in-depth and very informative documentary by Arielle Farve and Mckinzie McElroy. https://youtu.be/6XGmOQccuII

"A Brief History of BURKE ID Wallace to Burke Mile Marker Tour PART 3 of 4" by Ted of AuggieDogProduction is a wonderful tour of early Burke, Idaho, with the use of commentary and vintage photos. He also talks about the connection between the lead and zinc mines of Picher, Oklahoma and the Burke mines. https://youtu.be/Ey-KjopJ0Zw

"Wallace, Idaho" from Hoosier Jim's Travel Videos gives us a wonderful tour through the town where Lana Turner first performed on stage as a child, and where the best years of her childhood were lived. https://youtu.be/81qOxrmZQRM

About the Author

Cynthia Ackley Nunn is an author of historical nonfiction books. She loves a good mental challenge. Her favorite writing projects are those which require in-depth research to solve a puzzle or mystery, encouraging her readers to explore a topic further. Her thirty-five-plus years of experience as a researcher helps her seek out facts and bring clarity to the historical people, places, and events she writes about. Her other passion is photography, where she can use visual creation in both traditional and slightly odd representations of the world around her. Her favorite leisure activities include spending time with her family and exploring the natural beauty of the Pacific Northwest with her young granddaughter.

More by Cynthia Ackley Nunn

ABANDONED CALIFORNIA
KING SOLOMON MINE
978-1-63499-132-2

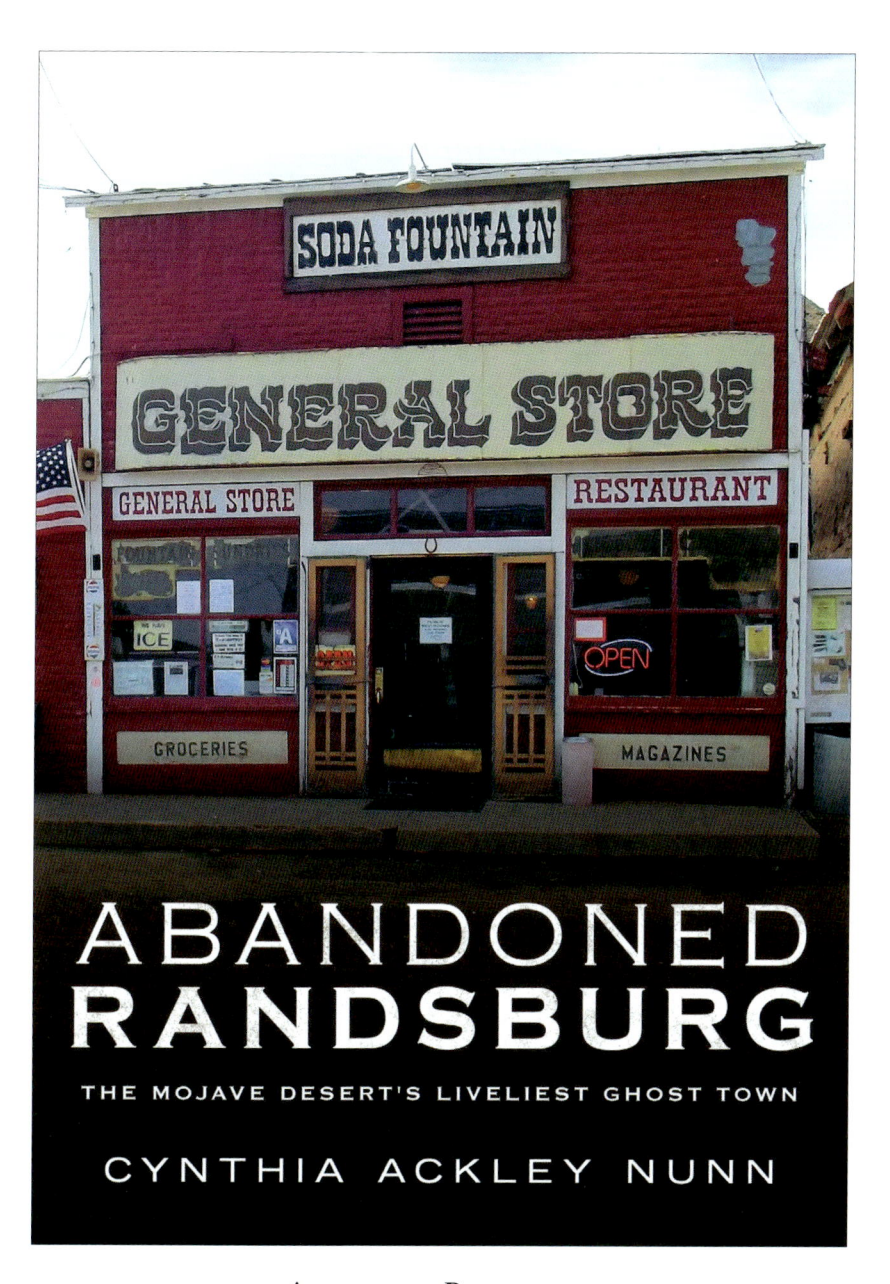

ABANDONED RANDSBURG
The Mojave's Desert's Liveliest Ghost Town
978-1-63499-135-3

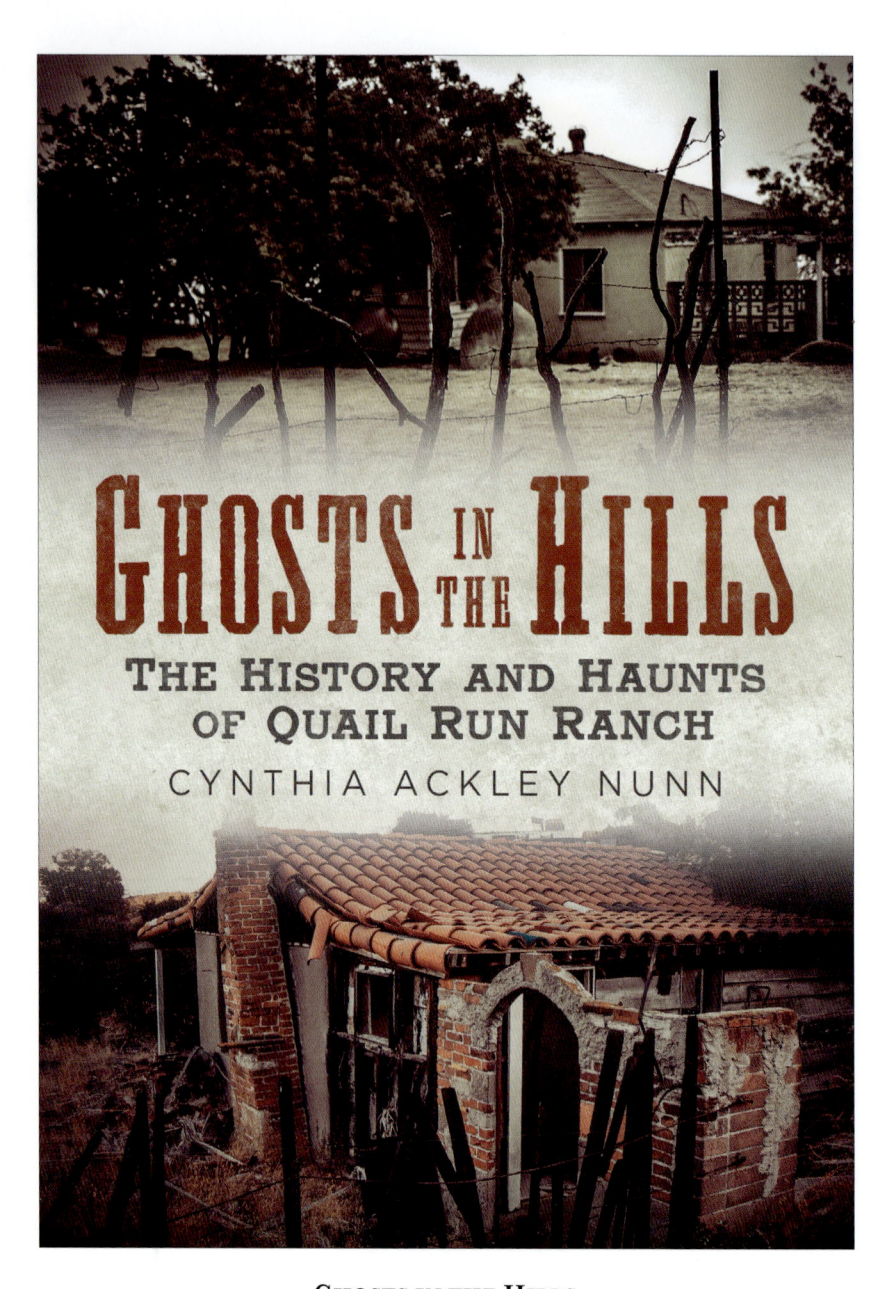

GHOSTS IN THE HILLS
THE HISTORY AND HAUNTS OF QUAIL RUN RANCH
978-1-63499-163-6